HOME

SAY Somthing

Table of contents

SPRING

Home (Spring) 8

Facade 10

First Day 11

Where the Heart is 13

A Home for You 15

Clay 16

Leaves 17

Sunset 18

Saplings and Glue 20

Magicians Hat 21

FALL

Home (Fall) 23

Monster Mash 25

Of My Dreams 26

Runaway 27

Vampire 29

Sleep 30

Behind the Drawer 32

Werewolves 33

Small Towns 34

Blind as a Bat 36

Patchwork 37

Jack-O-Lantern 38

My home, His home, Her home 39

Small 41

WINTER

Home (Winter) 43

Winter Song 46

When I was Young 48

Wonderland 50

Igloo 53

More than Walls 54

Earthquake 55

Among the Trees 57

Forgive not Forget 59

What I Want 60

Blood and Bone 63

The Basement 64

Lived, Lives, Live 66

Debt 68

Live to Work 69

Grief 72

Introduction

A home is not a house nor a house is a home

for while a house should hold a story

it's not yours to the bone

the place you decide should be truly your own

the moment you feel safest, that moment is home

SPRING

Home (Spring)

The blue jays chirped as they soared high above the flowering trees. The air was crisp and full of life. And as they strode down the familiar path they felt as though they could follow it with their eyes closed. They knew every slope, every branch, and every divot. They knew that no matter what happened, they could always find their way back here. Maybe that's why they loved it so much. Here, interwoven with the drowsy wildflowers and unhurried hawthorns, they felt truly safe. Walking beneath the trees they noticed the cheerful springtime flowers blooming all around them, almost as though welcoming them forward deeper into the bountiful forest. looking up through the sun-dappled leaves, the forest symphony ringing through their ears they felt, more than anywhere else, that this was home.

Facade

My home is not the place
I reside

four big walls pinning me
like a fly

while up in the sky my
dreams soar high

but the home that is
mine must be pitifully
shy

For I always call out to it but never hear back

show me yourself as the walls start to crack

my dreamy facade's crumbed attack

lets me know that a home must be something I lack

First Day

"Alright", I thought as I scanned the room. It was filled with snotty five-year-olds just like me, and I could sense their nervous excitement bouncing off the walls around me. But not me. I wasn't nervous to be starting my first of many days here, a long, grueling process of education that would make up the following formative years of my youth. I wasn't even excited to be in a new environment with so many possible new friends all around me. I was focused. I'd watched enough *Highschool Musical* to know just how to survive in this type of place, and I didn't just want to survive, I was gonna thrive.

My eyes scanned the room once more looking for the perfect target, finally locking in on a one girl in the corner, I'll call Blondie. She was blonde-haired, blue-eyed, and wore a lacy purple dress and pink bow hair clips. Perfect, this girl was gonna be my friend. In my defense I was never very good at social situations, my only knowledge of school and friendships having come from movies in which the pretty blonde popular girl always had the most friends and did the best in life. It had been drilled into me from a young age that to be happy I had to be popular. So that's what I strived to do.

I sauntered (or tried my best to) over to her, planning my next moves very carefully. "Hi!" I said in a friendly manner, "My name's SAY! What's yours?" I studied her cautiously waiting for her reply. "Oh..I'm..." she started before some lady burst in rudely with, "Blondie! I'm gonna go home and get your glasses. Are you ok to stay here?" Blondie...I thought. It must suck to be her. At least I don't have glasses. (As clearly if you had glasses you were a nerd and therefore could never be popular - again, *Highschool Musical* logic). But then, my new potential friend actually responded! "Yeah, I'm ok." Oh no. She *was* Blondie. I got away as as fast as I could but the rest of the day didn't go much smoother. By the end of the day, I had never been more excited to go home.

Where the Heart is

"Home is where the heart
is"

that must be true for me

cause all my broken
pieces seem to spread
out overseas

and I seem to build a new one with each new interest I
seize

Feels like a mansion all my own for everyone to see

but it can never be my own when there's still rent to
leave

With my landlord crashing down on me I must be so
naive

to think that it's sustainable to run off "I believe"

to tell myself it'll last forever helps the web I weave

I think the web will catch me but the strands are thin
as leaves

and the landlord holds the scissors though they leave
me the keys

I truly hope that one day myself, I won't have to
deceive

that one day all my own, I'll have a house to retrieve

A Home for You

you are home for me as I
hope to be

the one for you that
finally sees

all of you as all of me

drains away but at least
you're free

Clay

I hope that one day as I
crumble to clay

I don't let them reshape
me and instead, I say

My home is not the shelf
on which I stay

nor the kiln where most
ignorant lay.

I will not stay dormant or a malleable gray.

I will shape me, at least for today.

Leaves

my home is made of
comforting leaves

formed amongst familiar
trees

though at times, I fall to
nettles stings

I know this is the place for me

Sunset

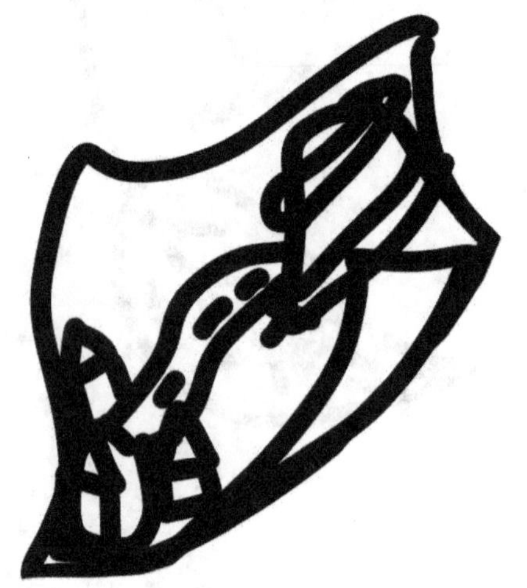

My hope lives on sunset

In the shaded perfect
trees

the leaves of winter all
grow back

when it's time for spring

My dreams live in Old Town

in the lights of the shops

Happy families working here

to grow their mom and pops

My strength lives on the hill

round and round it goes

I intend to end the spiral

wrap it up with bows

My hope, my dreams, my strength

they live in these banks

in the slope of these hills

in these rivers and lakes

In my small hometown

the family it makes

is stronger put together

than all of my strengths

Saplings and Glue

I made my home

out of saplings and glue

a makeshift thrown
together crumpled up
stew

And in it, I don't spend
too much effort to brew

cause it'd crash into dust
soon I knew

Magicians Hat

I live in a magician's hat

pulled from thin air just
like that

whenever someone
wants to chat

then poofed away when I
run flat

FALL

Home (Fall)

As they stride through the familiar grove, the leaves turn a faded yellow, orange then, finally, a brilliant red as they fall around them like the coming rain they could smell on the wind. They know a storm must be coming. As they crouch between the familiar trunks, sturdy and still, the leaves quicken around them and the first rain starts to fall. They beg the trees to stop the rain, and the wind, to keep their little cottage safe, to go back to how things were, but the storm was already in motion, there was nothing they could do. The cottage was built last spring on the idea that the forest would lie forever dormant on its drowsy windswept hillside. With the wind howling through their ears, the carefree symphony fading to memory, they realized things in their beloved forest would never be the same again.

Monster Mash

As night falls the raven
calls

the monsters trapped
within the thralls

Frankenstein cries

tied with twine

I'm falling apart but the witch just sighs

Dracula bellows not to whine

the lair of creatures haggard halls

can never feel like truly mine

Of My Dreams

The home of my dreams

how impossible it seems

It's right where I am

but with neat little
seams

Still here in my forest

but lacking ravines

though everyone says

that they're all make-believe

Runaway

I checked my phone battery, 20%.

I panicked slightly at the number but figured there was nothing I could do about it at that point. As I would say now, "Que sera, sera, What will be, will be." I debated for a while about whether music was appropriate and if it'd drain my battery too fast but I eventually decided on playing this one Auroa song I thought would be fitting. If shit were to go down it might as well go down gracefully.

Turns out that running for this long was hard. My ragged Converse and chicken legs were not built for this kind of exercise, and by now my ankles were bleeding from the blackberry tendrils growing along the side of the road, their branches reaching out to me begging me to come to my senses but I was too far gone.

I could feel my backpack ripping and cursed under my breath about the cheap quality, eventually, I had to carry it in both arms to keep everything I brought, my whole life until that point, from spilling out of it. That, I think painted a target on my back. along with my already "lost kitten-like" demeanor from the rain, The backpack slowed me down significantly, and by this point, I had stopped running.

A car started to pull up beside me, rolling its window down and trying to get my attention. I don't know if it was the exhaustion or adrenaline coursing through my veins that made me stop but either way, I wish I hadn't.

"Hey! What are you up to?" the man said and despite my deteriorating mental state I still somehow knew not to tell him the truth.

"I'm just on my way to a friend's house!" I replied and kept walking. He followed me for a while asking if I needed a ride and trying to convince me to get in his car.

Eventually, I had to pretend that my friend's house was just up ahead and run into someone's driveway to get away. He wasn't the only one that day. Swarms of creepy men pulled up next to me throughout the night with various attacks, all trying to get me in their car so they could take me to God knows where. None succeeded, but still, by the end of the night I wished, more than ever, that I could go home.

Vampire

My life is a vampire hidden away

deep in the coffin I told it to lay

to awaken only when stars are in play

to frighten the darkness and keep it at bay

Sleep

I sleep allusive avoiding
the fall

not allowing my brain to
recall

tomorrow's continued
brain-numbing drawl

until eventually I can no
longer stall

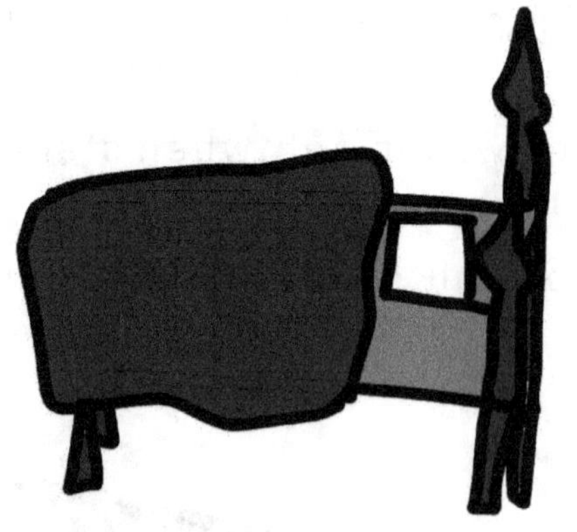

He sleeps angry remembering sores

making up lists for tomorrow's chores

always running the painful tasks that bore

cause through suffering he thinks he can be more

She sleeps anxious with racing thoughts

her stomach tied up in knots

till eventually she's seeing spots

falling to the sleep that her mind has fought

Behind the Drawer

I feel like a sweater,
threadbare and worn

my home behind the
dresser drawer

 Forgotten I was bought
before

my wear comes from the
moths and floor

A design fit for so much more

than rotting here so forlorn

but if worn now I'd be torn

so I guess I'm stuck behind the drawer

Werewolves

Sitting up against my
door

thinking what was done
before

werewolves turning to
their core

hiding here is such a chore

Small Towns

My lives have all lived here

I can't get away

the thing about small
towns

is that things tend to
stay

opinions, memories,

friendship and enemies

the grudges so hard to
sway

so I feel as I lay all the awkward replays

the heinous displays, the actions that weigh

filled with dismay I scream to obey

these parts of me so disobedient I say

they shouldn't have power but the more I push away

It's as if I'm spraying them down with hair spray

all the things I wish I could unsay

the texts that I've sent the games that I've played

but the more that I claim they have no place in my brain

the more I push and fill with disdain

the more power on me that they gain

Blind as a Bat

In my cave, I howl and
shriek

looking for the home I
seek

but the cold stone walls
are jagged and peaked

and the gray marble seems to shrink

Patchwork

My patchwork home, all
my own

each new draft chilled to
the bone

until the newest patch is
sewn

my threadbare home my
patterned tome

Jack-O-Lantern

My jack-o-lantern frame

holds so many old names

lives carved in before
each one changed

Stop! Not heard or so they claim

the candle can't light all aflame

My home, His home, Her home

My home is happy with
bright purple spots

with open doors and
pans and pots

for baking messes just to haunt

his cleanly walled-off organized thoughts

His home is dark and dull and strong

with big wood walls lacking song

iron cages contain his wrong

opposers here can't last long

Her home is light with things that bring joy

with decorations and pointless toys

cause what she says goes in her office decoy

she's too busy doing things she enjoys

Small

"My room's so small" I
tend to say

but the posters keep the
thoughts at bay

the brightly colored
walls console

the darkness right
outside the hall

glowing stars line the empty space

matching glitter that's encased

in the calming purple paint

I know I can stay here though it's quaint

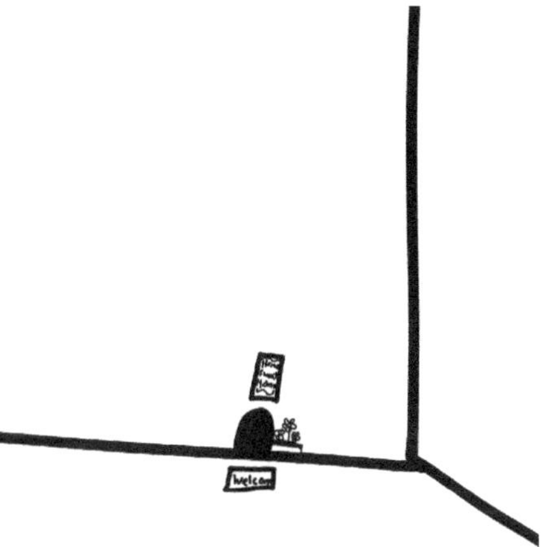

WINTER

Home (Winter)

The storm subsiding, they will rise from the soggy undergrowth, emerge from the mud and leaves they are trapped in, and looking around they will take count of their surroundings. Everything will look different, branches blocking their well-trodden path, the once cheerful flowers then shriveled and crushed beneath the ice and fallen trees.

But the trees, most of the trees will still be standing. While some may have crumbled during the weight of the storm, the ones left will be stronger than ever standing tall and proud to be a part of their forest. Their first instinct will be to climb high in the strongest one, to bring lumber and tacks and rebuild the cottage in the familiarity of their limbs away from the distraught, mud-laden ground that used to feel like home.

But then they'll know; they'll know that if the trees ever were to fall, they would come crashing down with the force of a hurricane, worse than any storms they have ever known. They can't make the trees their home. While they will trust the remaining trees with their life, they can't let them hold the weight of it by building their old cottage on the prospect of dormancy the inevitable change had left them crumpled. Like the flowers from the spring, the leaves from the fall, and then finally the crisp crunch of the ice beneath their feet as they walk along. Walking not back through their old nostalgia-laced path but breaking out through the brush to an all-new one. y walking they will see parts of the forest they have never known. In one, they see beautiful budding spring flowers in the seemingly evergreen grass that will make them stop to admire its beauty but after a while, they'll continue walking. Walking next into a forest with rain and apple-colored leaves falling all around them. This forest will scare them, but they will again stop to admire the deep oranges and reds of the leaves even noticing a couple have already turned a dark purple.

Then again, they'll keep walking for a while, walking through the next forest they'll shiver in the cold wind, but still stop to look into the gleaming snowfall all around them; then they'll realize even in the ugliest forests, in the bitterest cold, the terrifying unfamiliarity of the ever-changing climate, even when there is no beauty or comfort to be found in their surroundings when nothing in the forest seems safe or sturdy enough for the foundation of their cottage when everything around them is changing, they will always be home. For home is both temporary and permanent in its walls, for every cottage and every tree that has ever fallen, a new one will always emerge. The forest will always change even they, themselves are ever changing, but they will always have a place whether in dreams of the future, mindset, or physical abode there will always be homes and *they* will always be home.

Winter Song

As fresh snow falls, the new year calls

dragging me out from the thralls

of days gone past, fading fast

with promises built not to last

Lights all around the happy sound

of singing filling up the town

the new year calls the days gone past

the promises all fading fast

lights all around that happy sound

of winter song floating through town

When I was Young

When I was young, home meant to me

the people on my family
tree

the blood relations
being key

to comforting familiarity

Older though now I see

that home means more than family

the place in which I can be

myself with no hostility

That is where I want to be

a home built with but not on trusting trees

where I can feel like truly me

where I can feel like I am free

Wonderland

Alice was lost in a
feverish dream

led by a rabbit the color
of cream

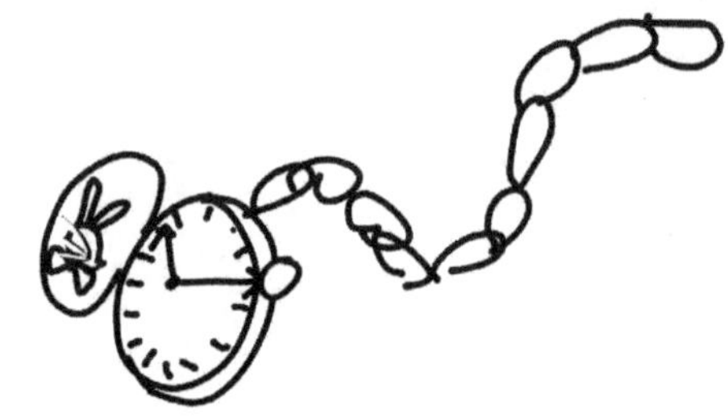

who, with time on his
pocket watch, was awfully mean

led to a state of which cannot be redeemed

I've feared the falling all along

the song of forever happy it seems

but I know in my mind I would be in the wrong

to fall into the frightening beams

But If I don't follow, I must find some way to survive

cause telling the rabbit he's wrong doesn't make me not cry

but if I play my cards right

I think I can make it through the night

If I don't give in to the aggravating screams

not be a puppet stung in the strings

I can say what I think though, I think that it's mean

cause if they want to control, I can too I believe

But now after a while, I've realized that I'm the Red Queen

playing the cards, lost in the game

and it makes me take a new perspective on things

cause if its all a game, I can choose to not play

But if I give up, what will happen to me?

Will the noise soon turn to comforting dreams?

Will I get used to the tightening seams?

And if I do, won't that brighten the beams?

Igloo

I live inside an igloo, locked in by icy bricks

surrounded by the solemn silence, watching the clocks tick

in my solitary fortress, I feel each second hit

waiting for the day, when finally the blocks start to split

More than Walls

Home to me means more
than walls

beyond the sturdy
painted halls

while logs and bricks can
always fall

my heart stands wherewithal

Earthquake

A home should not be
dormant

but ever-changing on its
stakes

in the case of a disaster,

it should flex but not
break

and if in the rubble,

after it's crushed by the quake

the thing is not to mourn

though it may be hard to shake

But instead, pick up the pieces

 acknowledging the ache

and know forming the foundation

may be a lot to remake

but don't let disaster

just ruin and take

cause if you're still stuck in the past

 another will awake

Among the Trees

My home then was in the
trees

hidden away behind their
leaves

until in fall their absence
grieved

I moved to somewhere
else till spring

My home is now among the trees

not frightened by the lack of leaves

now in fall, the absence thieved

for myself to feel like truly me

My home ahead still in the grove of trees

but not bothered much by rotting leaves

from fall to spring I never sheath

the part of me they don't believe

Forgive not Forget

Home are the people
that forgive but do not
forget

that love you
wholeheartedly but still
make fun of you for it

the people you know you
can trust with secrets

even though they know you're tired of their sh*t

What I Want

I want a home with open doors

with buckets for the hearts that pour

cause I want those who feel forlorn

to walk in and feel so much more

I want a home with window sills

so I can sit there in the evening chill

and when I get so cold I still

I can go back to heat that fills

I want a home with patterned walls

with dots and spots and checks and all

so that when I walk through the halls

I'm brightened by things that appall

Cause a home should be so much more

than endless bills and concrete floors

 as days turned chores and drawl and bore

a home should stand as truly yours

Blood and Bone

My home is built on blood
and bone

on ice and cold and
things unknown

one day I hope that I will
own

a house that's built on
memory foam

The Basement

My house has no basement, but I imagine if it did

that I would have really loved it as a little kid

that it would have been perfect as the place I would
have hid

but then again it likely would've been a place forbid

As I'm older now I realize how useful it would've been

to have a place to hide away the mess in storage bins

more than hide and seek or a cool underground den

but a way to keep all our messy secrets hidden

But instead the whole house is our basement with
echoing walls

with concrete floors and long spooky halls

I'm sure all our neighbors, as our house does recall,

the screamed out messages announced in our brawls

Lived, Lives, Live

I lived in my Grandmas
office

being there makes me
nauseous

nothing to do, eating
canned stew

and by the vans, I must be cautious

I live on my bedroom floor

propped up against my creaky door

with music blaring blankly staring

sitting here I'm never bored

I will live in a giant house

with noise and laughter all about

with purple walls and patterned halls

with nothing close to pointed shouts

Debt

The winter chill, the
debts, and bills

piling up on window sills

the snowflake song of all
along

building up what I've
done wrong

till fire dulls cold wind pulls

the collector adding up the tolls

the bills the wrong of all along

the tolls the pulls of winter song

till finally, it comes along

the new year here to clear the fog

Live to Work

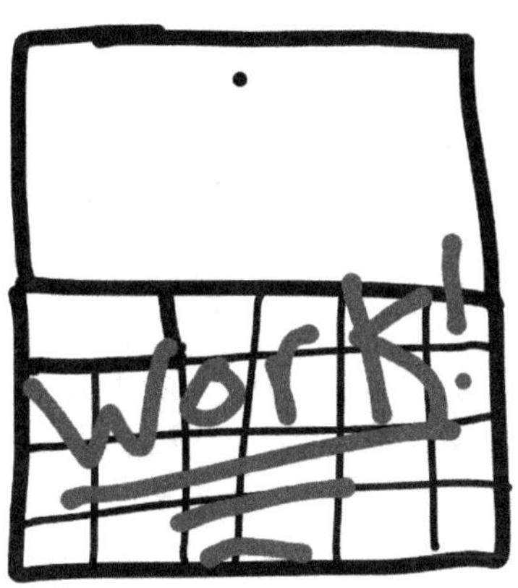

I talked to my dad today and the topic came up about work, I was complaining about off time. I had an event coming up and because of it I was saying how I would have two straight weeks without time to myself and how stressed I was about it, and he said this, "Well as an adult I can't relate, I'm on all the time. I don't get time to be off." I thought this was some kind of joke so I laughed a bit but he stayed serious, stoic, and still. So I asked what he meant. He said that as adults people don't get time to themselves, that they have to work their ass off constantly in order to support their families. I said, "I know that. Of course, as an adult, I would have to work harder, do stuff I don't enjoy, just like I do now, so that I can support myself and do the things that I do enjoy.

He said yes but that as an adult even during what he does enjoy that he is never off that in the back of his mind he is always having to plan and think about everything he has to do that even during the 30 percent of his day where he can relax and be with his family that he still had to focus on what was next on his list. 30 percent. That scared me, and so I asked, "Doesn't that make you sad? Don't you regret that the majority of your life is spent doing things that you don't like, working in a strenuous job all day just so that 30 percent of your life can be spent on your real life, yourself, your family, he said no, that he's proud to spend most his life working having the privilege to work so that he can have that 30 percent to be a father.

I asked once again, "Doesn't that make you sad? Don't you wish that you had more time, that you could be a father, that you could work but not spend so much of your life doing so. I understand that we have the privilege to work and survive; but don't you wish that you could have more than 30 percent of your life living it? Does that not make you sad that you can't have any time to just focus on yourself, your family, your actual life? He said no, that as an adult I would learn to live without it, without time to myself, without time being able to completely relax, to be able to multitask, to have family time, but still be working in the back of my mind on what needs to be done. He said that's just the way things are and that he was happy that things were that way.

At this point I was distraught, desperately trying to make him break, to make him show any sign of regret for how things had stacked up for him. I started crying, sobbing, but still trying to keep my composure. I told him that I didn't want to live to work but to work to live, that I wanted to spend most of my life doing the things that bring me joy, and that when I worked I wanted to work so that I could go home and be with my family and my friends, so I could go home and live my life not go home so that I could work the next day. He seemed confused. He said this shouldn't be a sad thing and that as an adult I would learn to live my life to work and be proud to do so, he was so happy he was able to do so.

I've thought about it now and I've decided that though it makes me sad, I don't think I can change his mindset. I know that he will probably spend the rest of his life working himself as hard as he can for barely anything or any fraction of life to himself until he eventually works himself to death. But, I'm not going to do that. Though I might work shitty jobs, or be in bad situations, I will always strive for more than 30 percent and I will never let myself be in a situation where I live to work. I will always work to live and no matter how much I need to get done or how hard my day is, I will always make sure that I keep the balance in my favor. I never want to wake up one day and realize that I spent my whole life working and that I chose work in favor of life.

Grief

Of course, I can feel at home

I know no matter where I roam

I will never feel alone

cause I will always come back home

But why doesn't it feel so

Locked in this room signs start to show

I'm restless, angry seeds are sewn

maybe I don't feel at home

But maybe feelings I can loan

Maybe this can feel like home

If I keep on doing what I know

I can make this feel like home

But I know those feelings are faux

true comfort I will never know

even if I act just so

I will never feel at home

Maybe this is how things go

I have a roof and grass to mow

though I don't right now, I know

one day I will feel at home

SAY Somthing

About the Author

Coming out of COVID-19, straight off the plane from Texas, and thrown almost immediately to the metaphorical wolves, SAY started high school prepared for pretty much anything. On an upward trajectory of mental growth and physical health, SAY started to branch out, finding new friends and new beginnings. Things were finally falling into place, and with his newfound confidence, he began to write. First just short poems about his past, into vignettes, into eventually publishing his first book "Gum Wrapper Poetry". With the support of his friends, family, and instructors, he felt as though he could conquer anything.